WALKING
in the
Graveyard

WALKING
in the
Graveyard

MICHELLE STEELE

Copyright 2011 by Michelle Steele
Published by Faith Builders International Inc.
De Soto, Kansas 66018
Printed in the United States of America
ISBN 978-0-9835998-2-1

DEDICATION

This book is dedicated to my husband and my children.

Philip, you have loved me unconditionally. When I couldn't see any value in myself, you loved me as if I was your priceless treasure. Thank you for being a man who walks with God. Thank you for being my cowboy. Por Siempre

Jessica, I am so proud of you. You have overcome every obstacle. Thank you for forgiving me for my failures. I will always be your greatest fan.

Gene, beneath your tough exterior you are such a tender hearted young man. I love your heart. I am very proud of you and the man you are becoming.

Angela, you are my drama queen. I love your sense of humor. You are a special young lady with a call of God in your future.

CONTENTS

FOREWORD

I will never forget the first time I met Michelle.
She had brought a man to the church that my
parents pastored in Goodlettsville, Tennessee. He
was in a wheel chair and Michelle believed that
God would heal him. I did not know her at all at
this time. After talking with my parents, I found
myself amazed by how God had delivered her. I
did not know that, a little over a year later, I
would marry her and we would begin an amazing
journey of faith that would take us places we
never dreamed.

Over the years, I have seen so many people
who have been tossed to the side and left for dead,
people who were walking in their own graveyard.
These were people whose cries were falling on
deaf ears because everyone had given up on them.
I have seen these people come to our church and
hear the life-changing message that Michelle

ministers. I have watched time and time again as their lives changed and they realize they are not the only ones who have been where they are. They discover that there was another in that same graveyard and Jesus brought her out.

I have watched as Michelle asked God to bring us the people no one else wanted. Then, when God sent them, she would meet them where they were, show them her past and point them to Jesus. It is an honor to be her husband, and her best friend.

As you read, be prepared to laugh and to cry. You will be shocked both by where Michelle was and the grace that delivered her. I know I was...and still am.
Good job, Honey, I love you.

Pastor Philip Steele
Senior Pastor Faith Builders International
April 2008

ONE

THE FORCE OF DESTRUCTION

Once upon a time there was a man who found himself in a place he never intended to be. Night and day the miserable existence that some called life inflicted such guilt, agony and torment upon this man that he took sharp stones and rusty metal to carve deep gashes in his skin that matched the wounds in his soul. In and out, among the tombs, stumbling in the dark he wailed a mournful, animal-like shriek. Hanging from his wrists, rubbing blisters around his ankles were the restraints of his friends who tried to stop his self-destructive behavior. No one could restrain him. The love of his family couldn't wash away the stain of his mistakes. The love of his friends didn't ease the burden of his guilt. The controls of his life were stuck in self-destruct mode.

"But when he saw Jesus afar off," Mark 5:6 tells us that he ran to Him. He began to worship Jesus. Years of guilt, shame and destruction were cleansed in a moment, and this man found himself in his right mind.

This story illustrates the pain of the first twenty-three years of my life. As a young, teenage girl, I made wrong decision after wrong decision. I made trouble at home, trouble at school, and trouble in my family. The real trouble was the self-destructing pain on the inside of me. From the age of fifteen until I turned twenty-three, I ran through the tombs and hid in the mountains of drug addiction and criminal activity. My family tried to pull me back to safety. I broke free from their love by lashing out at their compassion. I destroyed the relationships and the trust of the few people on this earth who really cared about me. My name is Michelle Steele and this is my story.

My teeth were grinding together. My jaw was twitching as I sprinkled the precious white powder into the cap of the syringe. I pulled up just the right amount of water and added it to the powder in the cap. I pulled the liquid cocaine into the syringe and tapped the air to the top. The sounds of the Sunday afternoon customers in the bar where I was secretly shooting dope were soon drowned out by the anticipated sound of the trains that came thundering through my head as my heart answered the call of the cocaine by pumping blood through my body at an outrageous pace. Add to the strong dose of cocaine, the fact that I had been shooting nonstop since Friday night. Perhaps, that is why I slipped out of consciousness before I could even untie the belt from my left arm. It could be why my heart stopped beating and my breath left my body.

Darkness surrounded me. Until, suddenly, I stood before a skull. The skull stood as tall as I stood. I felt hands reaching from the darkness grasping for me, trying to pull me into the skull.

In fear, I turned and ran. I ran back to my body. The man performing CPR on me was shocked. One minute he was desperately trying to bring me back to life. The next minute, he found himself fighting a frantic, panicked, half-crazed girl. I fought as if those hands were still reaching for me. I ran from the back room of the bar and down the streets of the inner city in Nashville, Tennessee. When my friends from the bar caught up with me, I stood bewildered in the middle of the street. The cold rain gently fell as I shivered in fright, the blood still dripping from my arm. I went to hell and hell was real.

I was in a graveyard of addiction. If you had met me during this "graveyard" moment in my life, you would have a difficult time recognizing me today. You might have looked into the dark, eerie tombs of my drug addiction and seen a wasted, hopeless girl. You might have concluded that this prostitute would never move beyond the street to make anything out of her life. No one that knew me ever expected me to make it out alive.

I wasn't born in this graveyard. Just like this nameless man, I once had dreams and ambitions. My mother and father both grew up and fell in love in a small, eastern, Tennessee town called Greeneville. My father enlisted in the Army soon after they married and took my mother to Maryland where my brother, Eddie, was born. A couple of years later, they found themselves stationed in Frankfurt, Germany, where I made my grand appearance. My mother tells stories about how I was the most beautiful child in the Army hospital. She insists that everyone could recognize that there was something special about me. Isn't that what every mother says?

I was still very young when my parents moved back to Tennessee. My father had completed his time in the Army, and we moved around a few times until we settled in Nashville. Dad worked with computers, and my mom stayed home with my brother and me. Life was good in my little kindergarten eyes. I loved my parents and thought things were perfect until I woke up one night to the sounds of my mother crying and my father speaking very harshly to her. I stood in the doorway of my room and trembled in the twilight as my perfect world began to come undone.

By the time I was in first grade, my parents had divorced. Soon, my brother and I were sent to live with my grandparents in East Tennessee. We lived there for about two years until my dad remarried. He brought us back to a suburb of Nashville to live with his new wife, Sharon, and her daughter, Nicole. Over the years, I made Sharon's life miserable. She was a strong woman, successful in her career as a physical therapist. She accomplished a great deal in her profession despite the chaos in our home. Nicole was a few years younger than me. She had a sweet disposition and was a better sister than I ever deserved. Life could have been so great.

As a little girl, I loved to sing and act. I loved to write and excelled in English. My family lived in an affluent part of Hendersonville, Tennessee, surrounded by country music singers and Grand Ole Opry stars. I visited regularly with my mom who lived in Nashville. It seemed like a normal, average life except for the self-destructive force compelling me. What should have been happy kept turning out sad. What should have been right kept turning out wrong.

As a little girl, I used to ride a Shetland pony on my granddaddy's farm. When I was about 13, my dad and Sharon bought a Tennessee Walking horse for my stepsister and me. I was thrilled. The barn was within walking distance, and I would spend hours there around the horses. There was an old man there, who was the caretaker, and he owned a mustang that had once been wild. That mustang would run like the wind. I was too naïve to realize that this man was using the mustang to get me in a compromising position. One day, he invited me to go with him to look at some wild mustangs he was interested in. He made it seem so innocent and fun. My parents let me go on this expedition, knowing how excited I was about horses. It wasn't until we were over an hour into our trip that I realized something wasn't quite right. The man was blurry eyed and slurring his speech. He reached over and started rubbing my leg and reaching in between my legs. I was terrified. All I knew to do was scoot as far to the window as possible and silently shiver in fear.

I made him angry. His anger was torment. He stayed angry with me for the rest of the trip. For a young girl that thrived on pleasing people and needed the approval of people, this anger became a heavy burden of guilt that followed me throughout my young life. What did I do? Why is he mad at me? My parents never knew what had occurred. Soon, I quit going to feed the horse and stayed away from the barn. My parents ended up selling the horse and I didn't care.

The next year, I started junior high school. Health class was taught by the seventh and eight grade football coach. We will call him Coach P. In class, he would let the cheerleaders or beautiful girls sit at his desk and help him grade papers. To a young freshman that wanted to fit in, it looked like a place to gain status. In the second semester, I was one of the "chosen" who sat at the desk to grade papers. Somehow in conversation, Coach P. found out that I loved horses and invited me to join him and some friends to ride horses in the snow. When the day came, I was the only one there to ride. Here we go again. Now what do I do? I didn't want to make Coach P. mad at me. When he began touching me, I cringed and screamed silently but didn't move. When he put his big moustached lips on me and kissed me I was horrified and tried desperately to think of way to escape this mess I had gotten myself into. I couldn't find a way out without making him angry.

I couldn't tell anybody because I was afraid that I would get in trouble. But, I was tormented. Finally, I got up the nerve to go to the principal. I sat in the outer office waiting to tell him, when out of the office walks Coach P. and the principal on their way to an afternoon golf game. I knew my words would be in vain. Coach P. gave me a warning with his eyes. From that moment something happened in my heart. I began to hate myself and a pattern of self-destruction began.

TWO

A DEAD-END STREET

Don't let anyone fool you into thinking that only poor people raised in the ghetto fall into a life of crime and drug addiction. I was a rich kid raised in the affluent neighborhood with my whole life laid out before me and, still, I fell into the dead-end street of destruction. My dad had promised to send me to any college and he would pay my way. I learned to drive in a Mercedes and had a car given to me when I turned sixteen. I had a pool in my backyard and lived in a gorgeous home, and still I turned down the path of destruction.

A dead-end street can be deceiving. If you miss the sign, you can drive on down that street like you are really going somewhere. And don't drive down a dead-end street at high speeds with bad brakes. You could find yourself in a ditch, over a cliff or drowning in the ocean. I ignored all of the warning signs. I was living life in the fast lane on a street that had no future. I never intended to be in this lifestyle. I never raised my hand in the kindergarten class when the teacher asked the class, "What do you want to be when you grow up?" and replied, "I want to be a junkie, a prostitute, a criminal!" How did I end up in a place I never intended to be? One wrong turn after another wrong turn placed me on this dead-end street.

The only time I had ever attended church, other than with my grandparents, was a local Baptist church that a girl in my class had invited me to attend while I was in sixth grade. I attended there for about a year, sang in the youth choir, and even went a trip with the choir to Panama City Beach when I was in seventh grade. There was an eighteen-year-old guy there who drove a black TransAm. He had a girlfriend, but he talked to me when she wasn't around. He was one of the few people who acknowledged that I was there. He called me a few times and wanted to meet me down at the barn where I kept my horse. Who knew that he was talking to me to get alone with me? I was thirteen years old when he had sex with me. After he had sex with me, he wouldn't talk to me anymore. I didn't go to church again for many years.

The inner turmoil of my shame and guilt began to poison every area of my life. I turned to music to medicate my pain and found solace in heavy metal lyrics that promised suicide was the solution. I immersed myself in the rebellion and anguish I heard in those songs. Within months, I found myself searching the utility drawer in the house for a razor blade and locked myself in the bathroom trying to slice my wrist. I managed to draw blood but didn't go deep enough to kill myself. No one ever knew that I had tried. While I still have the scars on my wrist, no one ever noticed the wounds on my fourteen-year-old arm.

I hid in the closet and prayed to Satan to use my life. I prayed for the devil to make me glamorous and sexy like the images I saw in my dad's porn magazines. I didn't even know how to pray to God, but I figured out how to pray to the devil through the songs I listened to and the books they led me to.

My parents began taking me to see a psychiatrist. I hated every session. Of course, he wanted to talk about the home life and my past and what could have happened to bring me to this place of destruction. I blamed everything on my parents divorce. I blamed my stepmother for everything going wrong in my life. I told everything but the truth. By now, I was convinced that something about me was bent toward the wrong side of the tracks. I ended up in the psych ward of the hospital when I was in ninth grade and began taking anti-depression medications. When I was released, I overdosed on them and nearly died. But, nobody knew. They just thought I was sick and needed to sleep.

I began looking for acceptance with the tough kids at school. Since we had never lived anywhere long enough for me to develop friendships, I had no idea how to fit in with anyone. I just tried to be tougher and crazier than the rest. I learned to drink the most, cuss the loudest, and take the biggest risks. My parents would drop me off at Rivergate Mall, and I would meet up with some older boys who took us out to get high and party. I lied to my parents about where I was going and went to concerts. I honestly don't remember any of the concerts because I was drunk or stoned by the time the music started. I barely remember the Van Halen concert that I snuck into.

During this time, I met a lot of older boys who took advantage of my youthful rebellion. It was easy for guys to get me to sleep with them because I didn't want to make them mad by saying no. Many times, a guy would make me feel like I had to go all of the way. If I started making out with him, he would pressure me to finish what I started. Little by little, I was being programmed to give away what I didn't want to give for someone else's pleasure. These guys made it plain that they expected something in return for the money they spent on a movie and dinner. But, most of the time I was never treated that good. I would just sneak out of my room at night and have people pick me up down the road. I became that girl that crazy enough to try anything.

I was crazy enough to run away from home as soon as I turned sixteen and got a car. I intended to go to California and get a job. I went all of the way to Phoenix where the boy who ran with me took my money and went back home. Someone gave me enough money to get back to Arkansas where a friend of mine had moved. In Arkansas, my parents tracked me down and took the car.

I got a bus ticket to Detroit where I knew a girl that I had worked with at the mall a year before. Detroit was a crazy, dangerous place for a sixteen-year-old runaway. It was in Detroit that I broke down and called my granddaddy. I woke him in the middle of the night. "Girl, what are you doing?" he said. "Get yourself back home!" I caught a bus back to Nashville. My return home was short lived because the next morning I was placed in a mental hospital for adolescents.

I was so mad that I had come back just to be locked up. I wasn't the only one who didn't want to be there. I heard a guy making plans. That morning another patient had become angry and slammed her fist into the window. The window shattered because it was plain glass instead of reinforced glass. This guy was talking about breaking another window and escaping that night. The girl who was my roommate didn't want to leave, but she was willing to be the diversion so that we could make a clean break. Late that night, the two guys crawled into our room. My roommate went to the nurse's desk saying that she felt sick. We pushed a bed in front of the door and I poured a whole bottle of Final Net liquid hairspray on it and lit a match. The guys picked up a nightstand and threw it against the window. The window didn't shatter like we expected. After a few more times of bashing the window with the nightstand, we were finally able to push it out of the frame and jump out onto the ground. We were on the run!

We went to an area in East Nashville where I knew some students of a diesel college. Party animals! I stayed there with them for a few weeks. The house was a typical party house with people smoking pot and getting drunk all of the time. One of the men that lived there had a girlfriend who was nearer to my age. I told her about my parents house in Tennessee and how rich my parents were. We decided to walk out to Hendersonville which was a full day's walk from East Nashville. We hid in the shed all night behind my parent's house and waited until they left for work the next day. We broke into the house and took jewelry from my stepmother's jewelry box. After walking all of the way back to Nashville, this girl claimed to know someone who could sell it. These guys took us to a convenience store on the other side of town and told us to wait there while they went down the street to sell it. They never came back. (Did I mention about how naïve I really was?)

I found out how to sell my plasma while I was there. I sold my plasma to buy a concert ticket to see Twisted Sister. Before the concert, I drank peppermint Schnapps for the first time. I got so wasted! I had drunk a little bit of rum that I had stolen from my dad's wet bar in our house. Beyond that, I had only smoked a little bit of pot and drank occasionally. I barely remember the concert. I lost the people that I had gone with, and I am not sure how I got back to where I was staying.

A few days later, I walked up to the shop that my Mom and step dad owned to say hello. This whole time I had been hiding just a few blocks from their shoe repair shop on Woodland Street. My mom was glad to see me. Jim offered to buy me a sandwich from the deli next door. I was so naïve that I missed their silent signals to each other. While he was next door, he called the police and reported me. At the time, I was really hurt to see the police pull up in front of the big plate glass windows. I felt betrayed as I looked at my Mom and realized that my first contact with her in months was going to end with me in handcuffs.

I left there in the back of the police car. I spent the night in the Sumner County adult jail awaiting an appearance before a judge. When I appeared before the judge, I requested that custody be removed from my dad and stepmother. The judge placed me in a group home called TRAC house in

Gallatin, Tennessee. There were about eight other girls in the home, and I settled in to my new life.

I went to Gallatin High School and lived in the group home for a long while. My grades were good, and I thrived in the structured environment. I joined the choral group of the High School and made new friends. I really enjoyed eleventh grade. I went to the junior prom and even traveled to New York City with the choral group to see "Cats" on Broadway.

But, it was during my time in TRAC house that I started getting letters from Bo Cosby. I had met Bo a year earlier through a friend in my junior high school. Since I was known around school as a wild girl, she thought Bo and I would have some things in common. He was so "wild" that while he was dating her he was asking her to set him up with other girls. The crazy thing is that she was actually doing it.

I talked to Bo on the phone a few times. At first, I thought, "What an arrogant guy!" He talked about sex. He talked about how tough he was. But, it was the challenge in his voice that pushed me to meet him. He dared me to prove myself by playing the "suburbanite girl is too good to come to East Nashville" game. He used tactics like, "You're too scared. You're just a tease. You're just like a Sumner County girl, all talk and no action." He was bold, dangerous and very sure of himself.

Bo was known around his part town to be the tough guy. All of the girls wanted him and he knew it. He had the rocker, bad-guy look with long, jet-black hair and steel blue eyes. He came in the room strutting around like he was looking for trouble. The guys around town were afraid of him, and the girls were intrigued with him.

I still don't know how he had gotten the address to the group home. He was locked up in a juvenile maximum facility for a robbery. In his letters, he talked as if we were girlfriend and boyfriend. He wrote, "I can't stand the thought of my girl being locked up." His letters came on a regular basis, and I was won over by the attention. I had never had anyone show any interest in me to be my boyfriend. We stayed in touch, and we ended up getting released about the same time.

The group home released me back to my parents. It seemed so difficult to be at home after all of the lies I had told and the distrust I had caused. I stayed there for a few months. My stepmother gave me a job in her company. They bought another car for me to drive, and we tried to return to normal. But the force of destruction was still raging in my life. I wasn't addicted to drugs or alcohol. I was just convinced that I didn't deserve anything good and determined to punish myself by pushing away those who I should have reached for. I was reaching for the ones who didn't care about me but wanted to use me.

I began talking to Bo on the phone and went to visit him at his grandmother's house a few times. The first time I went over, Bo was next door at his dad's. It wasn't your normal family situation where a responsible dad is around. Bo's dad would encourage Bo's illegal behavior. He sent me around to the side of the house after looking me over with a hungry look. His dad had an old bus that was turned into a camper. It was like a party house on wheels. Bo had paint around his mouth and was acting real funny.

I didn't know what "huffing" was all about, but I soon figured it out as Bo kissed me and his mouth tasted like harsh chemicals. He encouraged me to try, and I did it once or twice. After the initial hallucination, my stomach felt like I had ridden too many roller coasters and my head hurt. I didn't stay long.

He called me to come out again. I met up with Bo and ended up driving him around East Nashville finding pot and drinking beer. I had stolen money from my stepmother and stayed out without any word where I was. When they confronted me, I threatened to run away. I wasn't really serious. But, my mouth kept talking and my pride kept rebelling. My parents let me leave. "Just don't take the car," was their response. Bo was shocked when I showed up on his doorstep the next day or should I say, his grandma's doorstep and told him I had nowhere to go. We were sixteen years old.

THREE

DWELLING AMONG THE TOMBS

And when He had come out of the boat, immediately there met Him out of the tombs a man with an unclean spirit, who had his dwelling among the tombs. Mark 5:2-3

Anne Cosby let me move in with the understanding that I would sleep in a separate area and go to work to pay some rent. I went to work as a waitress at a restaurant down the street called Shoney's. One of the girls that I

worked with, named Tina, knew Bo and soon he
was going off with her when she got off earlier
than me. We argued about the fact that he was
spending so much time with Tina, and I soon
discovered that he was not interested in being a
one-woman man. Our argument escalated into a
fight and he slapped me a few times before
throwing all of my belongings into the back of
Anne's old truck. Anne came home, and when she
saw all of my belongings thrown in her truck, she
asked, "Why does he think he can throw you out
of *my* house?"

I should have realized right then that I
shouldn't stay with a man that would hit me. But,
I didn't have a clue about domestic violence. I
didn't know anything about abuse. But I had
nowhere to go and no one to turn to. I didn't feel
like I could go home or to my mother. Their
answer to my problem was lock me up or give me
antidepressants. My decision to move back in was
actually a statement. "You put your hands on me
and I allowed it and I'm staying for more."

I worked until close every night and tried to
attend school during the day. I dropped my senior

year of high school because I didn't know anyone. I went from being an A and B student in a suburban school to being one of the few white girls in an inner city school. I felt really out of place. On top of that, because I worked late I kept falling asleep in class.

Bo was going back to the juvenile detention center for about a year. He was incarcerated in a medium security facility near Pikeville, Tennessee, which was far from Nashville. We could only go see him about once a month or so. One day, Granny took me out on a Saturday and said she had a surprise for me. We drove up the highway toward an area on the outskirts of Nashville, called Ashland City. As we pulled off the exit, she told me that my surprise was that Bo was transferred to a minimum-security facility here close to us. We visited with Bo and found out that he could earn weekend passes for good behavior.

On the first weekend that Bo earned a weekend pass, he took some of the money I had earned to buy a $100 car. He worked on that pitiful car and got it running decent. The next week he called me and told me to drive up the street by the detention center very slowly. I knew what he was asking me to do and it scared me senseless. He had me pack my clothes and bring all of my money. I did as he instructed and drove up the street slowly, listening and looking. Nothing happened. I came back to Granny's house trying to act like nothing was out of the ordinary. Bo called as soon as I entered the house. "Come back up by the detention center. Drive slowly by the side of the road with your lights off and listen for me to whistle," Bo said. I traveled back up the highway and turned onto the road that led to the detention center. My palms were sweating and my stomach was churning as I turned out my lights and drove slowly down the street. Sure enough, a low whistle cut through the silent country evening and out of the darkness Bo and another kid, young and curly-headed, came rushing toward the car. They jumped in and slid down in the seats while Bo encouraged me to drive as normally as possible.

Now what? We are officially on the run with just a little bit of money. Bo talked me into calling

my dad and asking him for money to come to
Florida. While I hadn't really stayed in touch with
Dad, I found out that he and Sharon had divorced
and that he had moved to Orlando. When I called
my dad, he was surprised. He agreed to give me
money and let us stay with him for a few weeks.
He didn't even ask me why the big hurry. He
called a friend of his in Nashville who met us with
some cash and filled up our tank, and we headed
out across the country in an hundred dollar car
on the run from the police.

　　We arrived in Florida with big plans to get
jobs and get an apartment. At least, I thought
those were our plans. Above the gas money, my
dad gave us around five hundred more dollars to
get an apartment. We started looking for jobs and
checking out apartments. Bo wasn't able to give
his social security number or real name because
he was on the run. We were having a hard time
finding jobs.

　　I still didn't drink much or do any excessive
drugs. I smoked some pot here or there and was
satisfied enough. Bo had a different appetite.
While out looking for a job, Bo managed to

purchase some morphine and syringes. He brought them back to my dad's apartment along with a huge bag of "serious" reefer, and we sat around getting high instead of getting a job. My dad confronted us one afternoon when we were too stoned to even respond to his conversation. He told us to keep the money and find somewhere else to stay.

We packed our bags and left that night, not exactly sure where we would go. Bo had been locked up with someone who lived up in Michigan, so we headed in that direction. We came through Nashville on our way and stayed at a friend's apartment. We used some of the money that we had left over from what my dad had given us to get some drugs from the projects. This was my second experience with a needle. We found what was called "tees and blues." These two pills were used for heart patients, but we mixed them together and injected them. I remember that they were so "chalky" that you had to tear up a cigarette filter to use to draw the drugs through to avoid getting all of the chalk in your syringe.

We got high that night with Bo's friends and left in the morning.

With us was the young guy that broke out with Bo. He wasn't any trouble except when Bo wanted to have sex and then three was a crowd. The three of us stopped in Kentucky that night and spent some of our money on a hotel room. I was so tired! Bo had plans but, I was so wiped out that I ruined his plans. He was angry and mean about what he expected of me. Here we go with guilt and expectations again. I began to form an understanding that my value as a woman was based on the level of performance to a man's expectations. In other words, I was only worth something if I gave him what he wanted. The problem with this crazy dilemma was that "what he wanted" kept changing. I could never keep up with the demands.

We drove up to Michigan only to find out that the young man who Bo knew had went out of town to stay with his mother. The guy's father let us spend the night on the floor and made us breakfast in the morning. We had arrived in the midst of a snowstorm and had no clothing for the cold. The man felt sorry for us and gave us blankets and some old jackets as we set for who knows where. We drove until we ran out of money and out of fuel. We left the title in that $100 car and set out walking in the cold snowstorm.

I was sick and exhausted. I looked pitiful and felt worse than I looked. I was freezing on the side of this cold, wet highway wondering, "What have I got myself into?" Is this what I ran away from home to experience? I escaped the rules and government of my parents and school only to be miserable and cold in the middle of nowhere.

Bo called his family from the warmth of a truck stop. I remember him complaining to his mom that I was no fun. "She is sick all the time and only wants to sleep." His mother opened his eyes and mine to the facts of life. "Son, she is probably pregnant!" Bo's father agreed to buy us some bus tickets home and Bo's curly headed friend called his parents and headed home too.

Since we were still on the run, Bo's family prepared us a place to live on some property in the country that Bo's dad owned. There was an old trailer with no electricity or water on the top of this mountain in Ashland City. They fixed a wood burning stove for us to cook and stay warm and hung blankets as walls to keep the heat in one area. Bo's grandmother sent us some of the chickens out of her freezer that she had killed and plucked herself. She sent a box filled with welfare rice and tuna along with condiments and ramen noodles.

Remember, I was raised in the suburbs. I had done some cooking in our kitchen. I could follow a decent recipe. I didn't know how to start a fire. I didn't know how to cut up a chicken. I didn't know how to make coffee without a coffee maker. Well, Bo didn't know much either. Let's just say, welfare tuna and rice make the nastiest combination ever!

We stayed in that cold, dreary hideaway until winter broke. Bo went to work in construction so that he could get paid without reporting taxes. With his first paycheck, Bo bought a motorcycle to ride back and forth to work. While Bo went to work everyday, I was stuck on that mountain experiencing all of the changes that a pregnant woman goes through.

But, I didn't have anyone around to tell me what was happening. I didn't have any television or telephone to keep me connected with the world. We did manage to get some electricity turned on and had radio, lights, and a hot plate to cook on.

Bo wasn't ready for a family or any responsibility. Just like most sixteen-year-olds, he was ready to party. Even though we were "on the run," he became braver and braver about being in public and less interested in hiding out in a nasty trailer with a young pregnant girl who had no access to a shower or makeup.

One day, about three weeks after he had started working, Bo said, "I'm going to go get some hamburgers." I had only been off the mountain once or twice since we came back to the Nashville area. I was ready to get out of there. Immediately I jumped up, ready to go. Bo told me, "No, you stay here and I'll be right back." My heart wanted to keep the hope that he cared for me and would return. I kept myself busy for a few days waiting for him to return with his excuse or reasons why it had taken him so long to return. I would have believed anything. I learned to play the guitar while I waited. Bo had shown me how to play a few chords and his guitar was the only recreation on this lonely mountain. I remember that I learned how to play an Eagles song "Peaceful Easy Feeling." I waited an entire week before I walked off that mountain looking for him. I had run out of food and water and hadn't spoken to anyone in too long.

After walking an entire day, I reached civilization. I went to his sister's house because it was the closest. I was worried that Bo had been caught and put back in jail. Instead, I found him eating a peanut butter sandwich and sitting on his sister's couch. I was speechless-- and stupid. I asked him, "Where have you been? Why haven't you come back for me?" He never moved from the couch. He looked at me with disinterest and replied, "Don't you get it? I don't want you around."

I felt like I had been punched in the chest. I had lost my job to run across the country. I had risked my freedom to break him out of the detention center. I had ruined my relationship with my dad. I had suffered in a freezing, miserable trailer because *he* was on the run and now this. I left there and headed to his grandmother's house. All of my belongings were still there since the day that I had broke Bo out of the facility.

Bo's grandmother, Anne, was quite a character. She was known for her independence and sometimes her stubbornness. Above all, Granny was the advocate for the down and out. When Anne heard everything that had occurred, she moved me back into her home. "Just let him go on, then. You don't need him."

With the advice of Bo's sister, I went to the free clinic and signed up for prenatal care. I had to sign up for welfare health care for the birth of the baby. I had never heard of WIC and had no earthly idea how the welfare system worked. They had me sign up for everything. I had everything in place to receive a check, free cheese and food stamps, too.

I went back to work as a waitress at Pizza Hut and as a cashier at a juice stand in the mall. I worked my two jobs and saved my money. The next time I saw Bo was when he came by to see his Dad who lived next door. When I saw the car he was driving and the girl he was with I was infuriated. The girl who was now his girlfriend had been my best friend in junior high school! I am pregnant with his baby, and he's sleeping with my ex-best friend!

Little by little, Bo began making his way back into my life. He would drop in to the mall where I worked and order a smoothie to mix his vodka in. He would come by his grandmother's house and talk to me. Before long he was doing more than just talking. He began to figure out that he could have his cake and eat it too. Bo reassured me that this girl didn't mean that much to him. As a matter of fact, he had convinced her to work at a "massage parlor" in town. So while she was turning tricks in this massage parlor, he was out at the bars, drinking and having a great time. He continually came around while Cindy was "working" and he had sex with me. I was so desperate to have him back that I convinced myself this was just the first step to drawing him back.

I had been entertaining moving back to
Hendersonville, the town I had grown up in. I
searched and found some apartments that I could
afford with the money I had saved. I moved back
to Hendersonville. Because Bo still had the ability
to wrap me around his little finger, I ended up
with him and his girlfriend living in my new
apartment. Go ahead and say it: how stupid!

But, Bo had plans for me. When his
girlfriend was around, he acted one way. When
she was gone, he acted like we were still an item.
He began to drop subtle hints about how I could be
with him again. He started by telling me how
stupid it was for me to be working two jobs while I
was pregnant. He said that I could make more
money with less effort if I would go to work with
him. He had a new scheme in mind and little by
little laid out the plan to me.

FOUR

SOUTHERN COMFORT

It seemed like a soap opera, only worse. "How could I really be going through with this?" This was the thought racing through my mind as I stepped out of the car and made my way across the parking lot. It was a dead giveaway for a female to leave a vehicle parked in the "auto" section to go strolling down through the long line of eighteen-wheelers in the parking lot of the 76 Truck Stop. Of course, the fact that I was dressed in tight, black spandex that accentuated every curve of my sixteen-year-old body didn't help matters. I was afraid--of everything! I was afraid of the police, afraid of having sex with strange men and afraid of losing Bo forever.

Little by little, Bo had unfolded his plan to me. While seducing me with the promise of being "his girl" again, he revealed what he needed me to do. He wanted me to "work" at the truck stop with his current girlfriend, Cindy. He assured me that she meant nothing to him but he wanted me to play along so that he could keep her working. I convinced myself that if I played this game, I could make him love me again. I wanted the romance of that guy who wrote me letters wanting to protect me when I was locked up. The thought that should have been crystal clear, I continually shoved to the back of my mind. *How could you ever trust the love of a guy that would make you sell your body while you are pregnant with his child?*

Please realize that Bo never forced me to do anything. I could have stayed on my normal job, lived with his grandmother and gone on with my life. I realize, as an adult, the choices that I could have made at that moment. But, in the moment, I didn't see any other options, and there were no other influences in my life urging me to look at my responsibilities. Only one person "had my ear." If you are reading this and you feel trapped, hear me as I plead with you: Think about your future and don't throw your life away! Please find a responsible person that can speak some words of wisdom to you. Don't make permanent decisions in a temporary situation! Reach out from the circle of people who are pressuring you and ask God to help you see the bigger picture.

The first truck that I climbed into marked the beginning of a long, shame-filled road of prostitution. In the smoky, dimly lit cab of a truck, I began selling my services over the airwaves. My first "handle" on the CB radio became "Southern Comfort." With my young, sweet, little southern drawl, I would interrupt the trucker's talk to introduce myself. The saddest part of the whole situation was that as a sixteen-year-old pregnant girl, I made more money than the other girls on the lot. Cindy didn't like it that Bo only took half of my money and took all of hers. Maybe there was an advantage to being the other woman after all.

The first time I was arrested for prostitution was in the truck stop. I had been warned that a local police officer patrolled the lot and I should be on the lookout for any car lights when walking in the truck section. The first few times that I saw him, I was in the safety of a truck. The guys would hide me in their bunk as long as necessary. I even had guys warn me that the cop was driving through, and I would climb under the trucks or hide behind them. Eventually, my luck ran out, and I turned a corner and walked right into him. I received a citation and paid a $65 fine. The other working girls would joke that this was how we paid our taxes.

I stayed away from drugs the entire time that I was pregnant. When Bo and Cindy started shooting cocaine in the apartment, I became uncomfortable. Cocaine makes people act really paranoid and their behavior becomes erratic. I had never seen anyone mainline cocaine, and I was more than a little unnerved. At one point, he even tried to get me to join them. I became angry and refused. I wanted my baby to be born healthy.

I am so thankful that I stood my ground. My daughter, Jessica, is truly worth it.

The whole situation was built for disaster. Cindy and I didn't really speak to each other. Bo had crazy ideas about trying to get us to have a threesome but it wasn't happening. I had the only bedroom since it was originally my apartment. One night, he marched her right in, and they climbed in my bed. I wasn't impressed when he tried to pull my hand over in the darkness to join them. I stayed on my side and minded my own business.

Three was a crowd and soon his drug partner won out. I was getting too big to keep working anyway. Bo and Cindy went their own way and for a while stayed with his mom and her husband on the other side of Nashville. They kept busy at the truck stop at night. Eventually, they traveled to Florida with a guy who promised them great heroin.

I moved back in with Anne and began making preparations for the birth of my baby. Bo's family suggested that I call my mom and include her in the birth of my baby. I made the phone call and worked on repairing the relationship. I had already promised Bo's mom that she could be the one in the delivery room with me when I gave birth. I had even let her help me pick out the name of my baby. Her favorite singer was Jessi Colter, the wife of Waylon Jennings. She wanted a granddaughter named Jessi Darlene. I wanted to honor Anne for all of the times she had come to my rescue. That's why I picked out Jessica Darlene Anne for her name.

On the day that I went into labor, Anne and Bo's sister Melissa, had me walking in circles around the front yard. They said it would help my labor accelerate. I walked all day and into the evening. I finally went to the hospital that evening. My labor lasted into the night. For some idiotic reason, I had chosen to have my baby completely natural. That means, no epidural and no pain medications. By early in the morning, I was incoherent with pain and throwing up in the bedpan. Bo's mom left the room for a smoke break and my mom took her turn staying with me. Suddenly, Jessi was ready to be born. My mom grabbed the nurse and begged her to check me again. Within minutes, they were rushing me into the delivery room and Jessica Darlene Anne Cogburn arrived. She was beautiful and so dainty. Her features were so perfect like a living, fragile porcelain doll.

I took her home to Anne's house. I learned about midnight feedings and all of the fun adventures with a new baby. Bo's mother was the first to hear from Bo. She began telling him about Jessi and about how beautiful she was. She wanted Bo to come back to Nashville and put his name on the birth certificate as the legal father. Bo headed back from Florida. On the way back, he told Cindy, "I don't want you anymore." When he arrived back in Nashville, he acted like we had never been apart.

Would you laugh at me if I told you that I had hoped things would be different? Somewhere in my imaginary world, I thought having his baby would make me more valuable. Now, maybe he would want to settle down and be a family. About six weeks after Jessi was born, he told me about his new plan. I tried to talk him out of it and offered to go back to being a waitress. I wanted to be home with my baby. I wanted to have a real life. But, Bo had it all planned out. He said that we could get Granny or my mom to watch the baby. He wanted me to go to an escort service.

The interview process for my first escort service was the weirdest experience in my life. The owner of the escort service required a "date" in order to check out the services you could offer. I had to lie and say that I was single with no boyfriend because Bo didn't want me to be disqualified from getting the job. I made it through the interview process. Within the week I was equipped with a beeper, a credit card machine and my first "high-class" prostitution job. I drove myself in our junky car to exclusive hotels, climbed out in a sexy dress with a briefcase full of condoms. I pretended that no one knew what I was doing as I climbed into the elevator.

While I was working at night and sleeping all day, Bo enjoyed the benefits of my labor. He was free to drink, play guitar and shoot pool with his friends. He enjoyed the nightlife with all of the perks including sleeping around with whoever made themselves available to him. I knew that Bo was with other women, and I was powerless to stop it. If I had a night off from work and went with him to the bar, I was treated as if I was "unwanted" company.

While drinking one night, we started a game of truth and dare with another couple. We were out in the country in an abandoned trailer with a fifth of whiskey and too much time on our hands. The other girl challenged me to truth as she began to tell me how often she had been with Bo in the last few weeks. Bo became very uncomfortable because he expected me to turn on him. But, even in my drunken state, I still knew that I couldn't whip him. I turned on this girl instead. Bo and the friend with him were quite amused by the fight and kept handing my things to beat her with. As I held her down on the ground and beat her face against the carpet, all of the rage, shame and frustration of my situation was taken out on her. With every punch of my fists, I was beating all of the other girls that had been with Bo. I was beating Bo for using me and degrading me. We drove this girl back to town with her face bloody and swollen. The next day, her family came to the trailer park where we were staying with Bo's mom and said that this girl needed surgery to repair her eyes. I was the hero. Bo bragged about me to his friends and family, recalling every blow and reliving every punch. I wasn't celebrating. I was miserable.

My mother and Jim, my step dad, became very attached to my baby during this time. Jessica lived with them constantly. They bought her everything she needed. They outfitted their house and their shoe shop with all of the things a new baby needed. She had her own walker, highchair, bed, dresser, clothes, etc. They never complained about having her. If I came to get her and spend time with her, my mom was ready for her to come back as soon as I left the driveway.

Bo's family began to grow concerned and started warning him that my mom might try to take the baby. He became suspicious. Ever since Bo had heard about my mom calling the police on me when I was a runaway, he never trusted them. I was caught in the middle. The decision was made for me after one drunken, crazy night. Bo was blind-running drunk and I was well on my way. If Bo was happy before he started drinking, then he could be a happy drunk. But, if he was angry or upset when he started drinking, he became belligerent and dangerous. This was one of those nights. I couldn't do anything right. Everything I said was wrong and stupid. As we left one of the sleazy bars on Dickerson Road, he was going to leave me. He jumped into the car and I jumped on the windshield. As quick as lightning, he was out of the car. He punched me in the head and threw me down in front of the car. I rolled out of the way at the last minute before he drove over me.

I was unaware of the fact that he drove to my mom's house demanding that they give him the baby. It was two o'clock in the morning. Jim tried to reason with Bo. "You've been drinking. Jessica is asleep. You don't even have a car seat. Please come back tomorrow, Bo." Thankfully, Jim stood his ground and didn't let Bo take her. Bo became so angry that he punched Jim. The blow struck Jim so hard that he fell back into the house. Bo was afraid that the police might be called and left immediately. Jim never pressed charges.

I called my mom's house from a payphone on Dickerson Road, one of the most dangerous roads in east Nashville. I asked her to send Jim to pick me up. I told her that I was hiding from Bo under some vehicles parked in front of a business. She told Jim where to pull up and wait for me. When he came, I was so scared that Bo was watching from somewhere, that I sunk down in the seat to hide. The next day, my parents went to work, taking Jessica to the shop with them and told me I could stay as long as I needed. I think it lasted a day or two. I had nothing. Everything I owned was at Anne's house. I called Anne to talk about getting my things, and she started telling me to bring the baby and come back. She convinced me that Bo was sorry and that we needed to work things out. I went back and Jessica started being with my mom less and less.

Although my relationship with Bo was rocky, he began to lean on me and depend on me. In his own way, I think he loved me. When Jessica was a little over a year old, he asked me to marry him.

He proposed to me on one knee, in the middle of the dance floor, at the Starlite Club on Dickerson Road. He took the money that I had made prostituting the night before and bought a set of white gold wedding rings from a pawnshop on Gallatin Road. It was the moment I had been waiting for and yet it lacked the victory that I had expected it to bring. He wanted to marry me. But, he still wanted me to sell my body for a living. He wanted to marry me. But, I wasn't valuable enough for me to be his and his only. There was no beautiful wedding dress. There was no bridesmaids, no maid of honor, or best man. We got married in a courtroom, ate dinner in a cafeteria and went to a park in Ashland City to smoke some skunkweed. I was so stoned that I drove the car into a ditch. What a memorable occasion!

CHAPTER FIVE

BOUND WITH SHACKLES AND CHAINS

And no one could bind him, not even with chains, because he had often been bound with shackles and chains. MARK 5:3-4

As I strolled down the side of the road intending to look nonchalant and innocent, I scanned the cars for any sign of the police. I twisted my hips and flipped my hair as I looked for any sign of interest from the passing cars. Nervously, I took a long hard drag on what was left of my cigarette before I flicked the still-smoking stub to the street. *"I hate this!"* I thought to myself. My stomach was twisted in knots because of my nerves. But, I endured the anxiety for the hope of the high that awaited me. Bo promised that we would go straight to the projects as soon as I made thirty more dollars.

I wasn't used to being on Dickerson Road. Only the girls that couldn't make it anywhere else ended up here. This is where you end up when you have reached the bottom of the barrel. This is where the girls end up when they don't care anymore. I realized that I had crossed that line. I didn't care anymore. I didn't care who saw me here. Well, I did. I cried about it the thought of my kids in the car with Anne seeing me as they drove by. Even though they wouldn't know what I was doing right now, someday they would be old enough to know why Momma used to walk on Dickerson Road. I cried when I thought of my Mom or my step-dad seeing me as they drove down the street to run an errand. I knew that my family was aware of what I did. It was just that no one ever came out and said anything. No one had ever looked me in the eyes and said, "Michelle, are you out of your mind?"

From the age of sixteen, when I ran away from home, until this point in my life as I walked through the most degrading place that a young girl can find herself, no one had broken through the self-disgust and convinced me that I was worth saving. From the time that I began climbing into the eighteen-wheeler, semi trucks to sell my sixteen-year-old body for forty dollars, my belief system was strengthened in one thing. I believed that I was of little or no value. Even when I learned how to "dress up all in lace and go in style," the high heels and sexy lingerie didn't help the brokenness in my soul. I walked through the lobbies of the finest hotels in Nashville, Tennessee. I rode up on elevators standing next to the prestigious and elite, only to have sex with men old enough to be my grandfather for a few hundred dollars a night.

No matter how much money I made, I spent it all. My real drug addiction began after I gave birth to my first child. I was seventeen. Marijuana and alcohol had been the extent of my drug use up to this point. But, now I discovered cocaine. I started with snorting cocaine. Bo thought that snorting was a "waste of good dope." He taught me to mainline, and I was hooked. We would shoot cocaine non-stop for days. Once we started, we would keep on until all of our money was gone. Soon, we sold anything and everything that we could sell to keep on getting high. I spent two years of my life getting high day and night until I died. I mean, literally, I died.

I died in a sleazy hotel room on Dickerson Road. I was working for an escort service named "Charlie's Angels." The owner, "Charlie", found out that Bo and I liked to shoot cocaine and used us to "cop" the dope for him. We had been doing cocaine nonstop, eight-ball after eight-ball. I will never forget feeling the need to call and check on my child. I stayed on the phone with small talk and I was so high that I just wanted to keep on talking. I missed my daughter. I missed being a part of my daughter's life. She was asking about us because we hadn't stopped by in days. As I sat there listening to Granny tell me about the cute things my daughter had done, my husband pulled up enough cocaine for both of us into one syringe. I got off the phone just in time to pump up my arm as Bo let me know he would pull the rig out when he had given me my half. I watched as he methodically pushed the plunger all of the way in pushing his portion of the shot into my arm by mistake and that was all I remembered.

When my eyes rolled back in my head and the convulsions started, he realized what he had done. Charlie frantically collected all of his supplies and ran out the door leaving Bo to deal with my lifeless body laying on the hotel room bed. He didn't know CPR, but he knew that my heart needed to beat again. He dragged me into the bathroom tub and propped me up against the wall as he turned the cold shower on. He took his fist and started slamming it into my chest as hard as he could. After awhile, I started to breathe again. I didn't regain consciousness for some time. I remember waking up on the hotel room bed, soaking wet and numb. I didn't know my name or where I was. Bo took me for a ride to get fresh air until I began to regain my memory. The first coherent sentence that I could muster was to ask for another shot of coke.

SIX

UNTAMED

*And the chains had been pulled apart by him,
and the shackles broken in pieces; neither could
anyone tame him. MARK 5:4*

That night was a wakeup call. Bo was more
shaken by my overdose than I was. We stopped
shooting dope for a long time. He let me take a
break from prostituting, and we put an ad in the
yellow pages for a locksmith shop. His dad had
owned the Dickerson Road Lock and Key for
many years. Due to his drinking, he had let the
business run almost to the ground. Bo knew how

to re-key locks, open locked cars, and cut keys for most vehicles. We were in business for ourselves.

We went back to drinking and smoking pot as our social entertainment. Within a few months, I was pregnant with our son. We had a semi-normal life. We rented a duplex and tried to be a family. Still, there were the con-man schemes. Bo was always looking for a way to make it rich without working. He bought stolen items and resold them. Money was never put back into the business. We never had a checking or savings account. Bills didn't get paid regularly. I tried my hand at shoplifting during this time. We knew some people who would give us orders of things that would sell. I stole telephones, sheet sets, blue jeans, and stupid things that I wanted for my own house. I was arrested at Target as I tried to sneak an expensive telephone out in my purse.

My son, Earl Eugene Cosby III, was born on May 30th, 1989. This birth was different from the first. I had a great doctor that insisted on an epidural. I was more than willing. I had my son with minimal pain and got to enjoy looking into his bright, intelligent eyes. Bo was there with a camera. He held his son and was so proud to have someone to carry on the Cosby name. We called him "Hoss." The next day, Bo brought Jessica up to see me and the baby and brought me a joint. I snuck down to the bottom floor of Baptist Medical Center and got high behind the hospital.

Things stayed fairly normal until Anne cleaned out her safe. The year before I moved in, Anne's husband had died from cancer. Anne had hidden his medications in her safe all these years. I think she wanted to help us by giving us this bottle of dilaudid because she knew they could be sold for a hefty price on the streets. But, this sparked a whole new level of drug addition.

Dilaudid is a highly addictive painkiller used to help people through the final months of a terminal illness. In Nashville, it was second in demand next to cocaine. People who wanted a high similar to heroin could purchase a half a pill for thirty dollars or a whole pill for fifty. But, swallowing this pill was a waste of a good high. In order to get your money's worth, you had to shoot it. This took us back to the needle. We sold some of the pills, but ended up buying cocaine to mix with it to create a speedball. By the time we ran out of the pills in our bottle, we had developed a new addiction.

In order to get more pills, we had to go to the projects. We began spending every day in a vicious circle. We would spend all morning finding the first fifty dollars to get our "wake up" high. We would make a mad dash to the projects looking for someone who had a pill. Sometimes, the police were so thick in the projects that I would drop Bo off a few blocks away, and he would walk up into the projects and meet me back in a parking lot. Even though we knew that the police would impound the vehicle if you were arrested with drugs, we borrowed cars from his family and our friends to run our "little errand." They never knew where we were going. If we made or obtained any more money through the night, we would get high again. The next day we would start over again searching for a "wake up."

In drug addiction, I discovered nothing else matters except the next high. The reason I hated cocaine is that there was never enough. No matter how much you had, you were never satisfied. On cocaine, you sell everything you could get you hands on for one more shot. On the dilaudid, you would mellow out for a few hours, scratch your face and nod.

During this time, we started "playing the doctors." We found out from our friends where you could go to get some prescriptions of Valium, Adavan, and Tylenol 4 with codeine. What we didn't take, we sold. Between popping pills, shooting coke and Dilaudid, and smoking pot, you could probably guess where our money went. My mind was a fog of confusion and my life was a wreck.

During a cocaine binge, we headed to the projects with twenty dollars to find some more coke. A group of guys surrounded our car and while one guy put drugs in our hand another guy grabbed our money. The guy with our money started running and the other dealer wanted to get paid. Bo panicked and stomped on the gas pedal with the drugs in his hand. The dealer jumped in the window as we pulled off and began punching Bo in the head and wrestling with us while Bo was driving. There were two police cars parked on the side of the street. We pulled over. The dealer ran into the woods, and we were left there to explain what just happened. In my purse were two very large bags of what looked like weed. It was real marijuana. It just wouldn't get the average dope smoker high. Bo called it bunk weed, and he sold it to unsuspecting truck drivers. The police searched our car and we ended up in the back of the police car. Our cocaine binge was ended for the night.

Soon, I went back to another escort service to supply our habits and try to keep a roof over our heads. Anne was watching both of the kids now. Bo continued to answer any calls for locksmith work that came in. We moved from place to place. Sometimes we lived out of motels. Sometimes we slept on other people's couches. We rented different rat-infested houses and leased-to-own a few rundown trailers. We never stayed anywhere for very long.

One night, I received a message from the escort office telling me to call a certain number. They said that Bo had called and claimed that he was shot. I called immediately and Bo answered drunk and incoherent. He wouldn't tell me where he was. He wouldn't tell me what had happened. He just said, "Meet me at home. I've been shot." I went home and waited.

He showed up about eleven o'clock the next day. I was frantic. Sure enough, he had been shot twice. One bullet had passed clean through the fleshy part of his side. The other bullet, he claimed to have taken out himself. He wouldn't tell me where he had been or what he had done to get shot at. He was wrapped tight with gauze but he had not visited a hospital. I never found out what had happened. The next day he received a call to re-key all of the locks in a huge house. I remember that he lost a lot of blood as he worked on that house. When we got paid for the job, I was stunned to see the name on the check. We had just re-keyed the locks in the house of Garth and Sandi Brooks while Bo was bleeding from a gunshot wound.

By this time, my heart was growing colder and harder. We had fought many times and I left him. But I was too afraid to actually leave town. He threatened that I would never see my kids again.

He, often, swore to kill me if I found another man. One time that I had left him, he found me in a motel that I had rented by the week. I took a handful of purple Valium as he walked in the door. He talked in a deceptively sweet voice as he looked through the room to see what I had been doing. I was calm, very calm and let him talk. My inner voice kept coaching me. "Stay calm and he won't hit you. Don't give him any reason to get mad." He found a knife over by the wet bar. It was a brand new kitchen knife that I had stolen. He grabbed that knife as he choked me against the wall laying the edge of the blade against my face. Speaking through clenched teeth, he threatened to kill me. I was so numb from the Valium and from the misery of my life I answered, "I don't care. I really don't care anymore." This was the first time that I had not tried to fight back. This was the first time that I didn't have a look of stark terror in my eyes. In actuality, I was too mellow from those drugs to lift my arms. He dropped the knife as the blood started to pour from an inch, long cut on my left cheek. Although this cut should have had stitches, I just bandaged it and

sat back down. Suddenly, he was sorry. He began
to apologize and ask me to come back to him. I
just said, "Whatever." I had hit the bottom.
Something in me had snapped. I really didn't
care.

SEVEN

CRYING OUT IN SELF-DESTRUCTION

And always, night and day, he was in the mountains and in the tombs, crying out and cutting himself with stones. MARK 5:5

I became pregnant again. This time I wasn't sure who the father of the baby would be. I had been pressured a few times by different clients to have sex without a condom. If the price was right or if they offered me drugs as an incentive, I gave in. Also, rubbers weren't always effective and more than one had broken. My drug activity had interfered with my birth control pills and now I was pregnant. I found an abortion clinic and scheduled an appointment. I didn't tell Bo about my uncertainty. I just told him that we couldn't handle another baby right now. We weren't raising the children that we had. He didn't care. He dropped me off at the abortion clinic like he was dropping me off at the mall. I filled out the paper work and sat for a few minutes in the waiting room. When the nurse called me back to the room, she gave me a Valium. I thought, "Just one?"

I was sick in my stomach because of the choice that I was about to make. I wanted something to numb the pain in my heart that was present with me every waking moment. Instead, that pain grew until I felt a bitter self-hatred welling up inside me. I just wanted to get this over with. I disrobed from the waist down and positioned my feet in the stirrups like I had done a dozen times before for a pap smear. From the time the doctor came into the room until the time he left was less than five minutes. As he pulled the lifeless baby out, I could feel the warm body as it slipped through what should have been the birth canal. Instead it was a death canal. I realized too late that life has no rewind and some choices you can't take back.

Since I couldn't work for a few weeks, and we didn't have much money, Bo and I drove to where his mother, Pat, was living in West Tennessee. The kids came down too when Bo's sister, Melissa, came down for a visit. Pat had a small trailer on a large piece of land in the middle of the country. We didn't tell her about the abortion. Bo just acted like we had come to stay for a while. I was depressed and didn't want to be there at all. The country life didn't last long. We ran out of the pot supply and the prescriptions that we had carried with us. I had a fit and left with the kids in one of the cars that we had taken. I was halfway back to Nashville when the fuel gauge started showing empty. I pulled over and called Bo's mother. She said that he was right behind me. He caught up with us and fueled the car back up and we came back to Nashville together.

I began living my life with a determined purpose. I was determined that I would never be sober another day in my life. I got high as a survival instinct. A sober day was not an option. I had become the walking dead. I was walking through each day, lifeless on the inside. If I couldn't get high, I would get drunk. I didn't even like to drink! But, it was preferred over being sober enough to feel my shame, my regret, and my bitter self-hatred. If I couldn't get drunk, I would drink a whole bottle of Nyquil. Sometimes, I had to steal the Nyquil because I was so desperate to forget the pain.

At one of the lowest, most tumultuous moments in my life, I emptied another prescription bottle into my stomach. This time, I almost succeeded in killing myself. It happened during a time when I was learning to shoot cocaine without Bo's help. I was given some cocaine that either had hallucinogens mixed with it or maybe was more pure than I had ever mixed before. I was seeing things and very paranoid. I was driving my old van down Gallatin Road in Madison and I thought Bo and his friend were on the van playing tricks on me. I kept stopping the van in the middle of the road, climbing out, and running around the van screaming at him to leave me alone. I was terrified that he would catch me doing drugs without him. At the same time, I was mad at him because he had been sending me to "work" at an escort service and getting high while I was gone.

Anyway, the tainted drugs mixed with my fear of him and anger at him made for a volatile mixture. By the time I reached the apartment complex, I was convinced that he was on the roof of the van. I could hear him laughing at me and taunting me. I was seeing things that looked like aliens. They were jeering at me. But, I assumed that they were really Bo and Lee following me.

My rage boiled over as I pulled into the parking lot, and I rammed into his vehicle—a beautiful, royal blue, Spyder convertible. I wasn't through. I backed the van up and punched the gas, smashing into his car over and over again. I don't know if I parked the van or not. I remember walking into the apartment to find him sitting on the couch. Now, I was really scared. But, he had no clue what was going through my mind. I went straight to the bathroom, grabbing a full prescription of ninety Adavans from the vanity counter on my way. I swallowed the ninety pills and walked out into the living room. I threw the empty bottle at him and ran.

I remember running into a wooded lot where I had to crawl on my hands and knees under bushes and through thick shrubs. I was terrified to be caught by him. Someone found me passed out in a driveway. An ambulance carried me to the emergency room and pumped my stomach. Bo found me in the emergency room and smuggled me out because he knew that they would admit me in the psychiatric ward. I don't remember anything beyond crawling through the thick brush. A great deal of the medication had absorbed into my system. He told me later that I was hysterical, fighting and demanding that he let me go.

He let me get out of the car and I went my own way. I only remember pieces of the next three weeks. I ended up being used by another pimp who was making me steal from the tricks. This guy kept me high and kept me hidden in a miserable, rat-hole of a motel named Town Court. My husband came looking for me and heard that Big Jim had me in Town Court. He came packing his pistol and dragged me out of there.

Still, I was silently fuming about the gunshot. I was beginning to realize that there was more going on while I was working than I knew about. When I worked, he took all of my money to use on drugs. But, he was getting high without me and I wasn't getting any of it. I began putting two and two together, and I began to voice my opinion. He never admitted it. But, he never denied my suspicions. I confronted him. "It is not fair that you are pulling robberies or stealing whatever you are stealing and you don't give me any of the money or drugs. But, you take my money and spend it how you want!"

His response was, "Fine, get in the car." He had been hanging out with a guy named Allen. Allen had been in the house when our fight started. He was in his car waiting on Bo. As we walked out and got in the car, Allen followed the directions that Bo gave him. We ended up at a convenience store. Bo climbed out of the passenger side and motioned for me to climb out of the back seat. I was still pouting and had my arms crossed as he told me what to do. This was not what I meant! I meant he should share with me what he got, not make me do it with him! I didn't want to rob a store.

We walked in together, and I just stood there glaring at him. He walked to the beer coolers, grabbed a twelve pack and went to the counter. He looked down and saw a Doberman behind the counter next to the cashier and walked out. We got back into the car, and he told Allen which store to go to next. We ended up in Madison at a Delta Express gas station on Gallatin Road. I stayed in the car this time. Bo pretended to have a gun and came running out with under twenty dollars. We headed to the projects for dope. On the way, he hit one more gas station. We ended up with less than fifty dollars. This wasn't what I wanted. I didn't want either of us to go to prison. I didn't want him to rob gas stations.

We were apprehended two blocks from the projects. The police pulled us out of the car and handcuffed us. Bo was charged with the robberies. Allen turned states evidence, which means he was offered a deal for testifying against Bo. They charged me with attempted armed robberies. I was released without bond. Bo asked me to go back to the streets prostituting until I could get enough money to post his bond. It took me awhile because I was stopping to get high. He kept calling his grandmother's house collect from the Davidson County Jail wondering what was taking me so long. I finally had enough, and he was released on bond until our court date.

We took a bus down to West Tennessee where his mother was still living. He was talking about us running to Canada. That decision would mean that I would be separated from my children forever. I would have to take on a new identity and live like my children never existed. I cried bitter tears as we traveled down toward Jackson.

EIGHT

LEFT ALONE IN THE GRAVEYARD

Have I mentioned the fact that I loved Bo Cosby? As messed up as Bo was, in his own sick twisted way, he loved me. In my own sick and twisted way, I loved him too. My mom later told me, "Michelle, I knew that you were just as addicted to Bo as you were to drugs. I knew you'd never stop without him." She was right. I couldn't live with him and I couldn't live without him. Just like hundreds of other women who get beaten and mistreated, yet they stay with the one who hurts them, I was convinced that I couldn't make it without him.

I was relieved when Bo gave up on the idea of running away to Canada. I was surprised when he started preparing himself to do his time. Our time back in the countryside was long enough for Bo to put some things in perspective. He decided to come back and face his sentence. When he came back, he talked to the prosecutors to plea bargain for my charges to be dropped. If he went through with it, I would walk and he would serve eight to ten years in the state penitentiary. I wasn't sure what to think.

During the time that we were waiting for the sentencing, we still fought. He was ready for this great turnaround. He wanted me to get a regular job after he went in and quit doing drugs. He wanted me to live with his grandmother and raise our children. All of these things would have been exactly what I was hoping to hear six or seven years ago. But, after years of selling my soul, I didn't think I could be normal again. After years of medicating my shame with a syringe, I didn't know if I could escape the "Hotel California." Do you remember the song? It says, "You can check out anytime you'd like, but you can never leave."

Of course, he still wanted me to "work" right now because we needed money for the lawyer. After I got off work at the escort service, I started going by the bar where a guy who had cocaine would supply me. The bar was closed, but the guy was the owner and he lived in the back. I was paranoid about Bo catching me, but my need for the needle drove me to do it. After a few hours there, I would catch a cab back to Bo's grandmother's house where we were living until our trial.

After a disagreement, I didn't come back for about four days. I worked at the service at night and went different places during the day. His mother called the escort service with an urgent message that I call her. I called in between tricks to find out what she wanted. Pat begged me to come back to Bo. She told me that he loved me and was sorry for the way our lives had turned out. She said he was a mess without me and really needed me. It was all the things I wanted to hear him say, not his mother. I waited until the next day. But, I went back.

His attitude was different. I quit working and stayed around with the kids and the rest of the family as we waited to appear in court. Court was scheduled for a Monday morning. Bo promised Anne that he would go to church with her on Sunday. That Sunday morning, Anne took the kids and went to church like she did every Sunday. Bo woke up late and scrambled around to get ready. I was shocked that he would really go. He tried to convince me that I needed to go too. I told him he was out of his mind! I went through all of the excuses about the walls caving in and lightning striking the building. I didn't go. I stayed at the house by myself.

When they all came bouncing in the house, they were thrilled and excited. The kids were jumping up and down and Anne was smiling ear to ear. Bo was even unusually happy for someone that was facing ten years of prison time. Anne announced to me that Bo had gotten saved. I wasn't sure what that meant so, they explained to me that Bo had went up to have the pastor pray for him and he had asked Jesus to save him. I still didn't know why that was such a big deal.

Bo had a cassette tape that somebody at the church had given him. It was some blues music that one of the guys who prayed for him had made. Bo liked it and was listening to it throughout the day. He asked me to read the Bible to him since he couldn't read very well. I rolled my eyes and started reading. I wasn't impressed with all of this Bible stuff and music about a glory train.

The next day, we faced the music. As we walked into the courthouse, we were all a bundle of nerves. We were in the hallway waiting for our place on the docket when one of Bo's friends came up. I thought that it was really nice of him to come show us that support. I turned around and they had disappeared. No one knew where Bo was. Fifteen minutes later, Bo returned. He said they had gone to the bathroom. In reality, he had gone to a bathroom on another floor because his friend wanted to "help him out." His friend placed a morphine patch on his side. This patch was the size of a piece of notebook paper and worked like a nicotine patch would work. It was something experimental and was being used on cancer patients in their last stages. His friend thought they would probably take Bo in custody and this patch would keep him high for the first few days of processing. It had enough morphine to time-release over three days.

They sentenced Bo and accepted the plea bargain. The judge announced that he had a number of days to put his affairs in order since he was out on bond. We left the courtroom relieved that we had a few more days before he had to report to intake. By the time we left, Bo was beginning to feel the effects of the morphine. He still hadn't told me about it. He let me in on his secret that evening when he was nodding out in mid-sentence. The only drug that I had indulged in for weeks was pot. Bo offered to cut the patch in half and put half of it on me. I tried to get him to pull it off and let me wear it for a few hours. But, he wanted to keep the high he had going. So, he cut off half of the patch and gave one side of it to me.

I never felt a thing. I waited for the least little feeling but there was nothing. I reassured myself that I could go the next day and get something. It was too late to do anything that night. Bo enjoyed the Christian blues music and made me read the Bible to him some more. He went to bed and slept hard through the night.

In the morning, he was still sleeping hard. I had to climb over him to get out of the bed and I didn't even wake him up. That was unusual. He was a light sleeper. He was still snoring like a rock. I assumed it was the morphine making him sleep harder than usual. I got myself dressed for the day and helped Anne with the kids. I was ready to go get something for myself so I kept trying to wake him up by making noise in the room. I was willing to put up with him being angry with me for waking him up. I let our four-year-old son wander in with his out-of-tune guitar and began to "play" while he shouted the words to Rocky Top at the top of his lungs. I started the vacuum cleaner and vacuumed the floors in every other room and finally ended in his room. Finally,

I turned the vacuum off and turned around to wake him up.

Bo wasn't even breathing. I called his name and shook him. Still, he wasn't breathing. Hoss was still on the floor. Anne was in another part of the house. I began screaming for her to call an ambulance. The fire station was at the end of the street. They could be here quickly.

I tried to remember everything I had ever heard about CPR. I tried to breathe into his mouth. The air I pushed in with my breath just came bubbling back out of his mouth into my mouth. It didn't even seem to enter his lungs. I tried to stand over him and push on his chest. The bed was so soft that his whole body just bent into the bed. So, I tried to pull him onto the floor. His head hit the nightstand and his body was tangled up in the sheets. He was covered in sweat and I couldn't get a good grip. I started to cry in desperation. I started talking to him. "Don't you die, Bo Cosby!"

Within minutes the paramedics came rushing in and moved me out of the way. Anne pulled the kids into the back room and called down the street where Bo's sister and Mom were. They pulled up in front of the house as Bo's body was being lifted into the ambulance with the paramedics still working to revive him. I was in the front seat as the ambulance sped toward Memorial Hospital about eight minutes away. I answered their questions and tried to explain about the morphine and the time released patch.

They escorted me to a private waiting room and, as Bo's family began arriving, they brought them to this private room. We began reassuring each other that everything would be okay. I tried to explain the morphine and the time-released patch to the family. We assumed that they would just revive him and everything would be fine. Then, a woman counselor from the hospital arrived to talk with us. Slowly, we began to realize that this condition was more serious than we had thought and the hospital was sending us someone to help us if he died. I will never forget the look on Pat's face as she asked the question that we all were afraid to ask. "So, isn't everything okay now that you have resuscitated him?"

The counselor began to explain that Bo had
been without sufficient oxygen throughout the
night. The morphine patch had released three
days of morphine into his body in one day. His
diaphragm was unable to expand adequately.
That was the noise that I mistook for snoring. He
had been struggling to breathe! I had been
selfishly thinking about myself while he was
struggling to hang on to life.

We were moved up to the intensive care
waiting room. Bo was only living because of the
machines that kept his body alive. We were only
allowed to go into the room with Bo a few times a
day for a few hours. Family members and people
from Anne's church came to visit us. Soon, our
friends heard about it and came to the hospital.
Some people thought that Bo had committed
suicide to avoid prison. Everyone was in a state of
shock.

Some of our friends came up to the hospital
and brought me something to help me "cope." One
girl took me into the bathroom and gave me a
Dilaudid and a syringe. I felt guilty as I took my
place back in the waiting room next to Bo's family

with my face itching and my eyes nodding. But the guilt was short lived. My friend came every day and helped me out. I kept the syringe in my shoe and when the guy from the bar called and asked me if I needed anything, I asked him to bring me some coke so that I could stay awake.

Bo's condition had not improved. As a matter of fact, his brain was swelling. You could visibly see the area around his temples and his eyes protruding. The doctor called the immediate members of the family together for a meeting. He explained that Bo was brain dead and had suffered so much brain damage that he would be a vegetable for the rest of his life. He gave us the option to unplug the machines and let him pass away or keep him plugged up to the machines indefinitely in a coma.

It was during this time that the man from Anne's church who had prayed with Bo on the Sunday he had attended church, came to the hospital. This was the man who had played the Christian blues music that Bo had been listening to. I had never met him before and he wasn't what I expected to see from the church. He was wearing a black, leather biker's vest and wore a long ponytail down his back. His face was covered in a thick beard, and he carried a huge, worn, black Bible. His name was Zach and he said that he wanted to pray for Bo because he believed that God would heal him. I didn't think his prayer would do any good. Still, I asked Pat if she cared that this man prayed for Bo. She didn't seem to keen on the idea either. It sounded far out to both of us, but we took him back. We let him pray and prayed with all of his might. Personally, I was caught between feeling uncomfortable and feeling sorry for this guy.

He went back to the waiting room with us and began to talk to me about my life. I skirted around as many questions as I could until finally he suggested that we go to the chapel and talk. I didn't want to go the chapel, and I didn't want to talk. This man was insistent. He kept on until I agreed to go. As we walked out of the waiting room, my friend from the bar was walking up the hall. I tried to get out of the chapel meeting, but Zach said he would wait. I walked to the other end of the hall with the friend from the bar and he slipped me a twenty-cent piece (twenty dollars worth) of cocaine.

What a mess! My husband is being kept alive by machines. The doctors say there is no hope. Some biker/preacher wants to pray with me in the chapel. I have a syringe in my shoe and cocaine in my pocket. I repeat, what a mess!

I went to the chapel and listened to Zach. Well, I was halfway listening. He was insistent and continued to ask questions that made me think. He was determined to get through to me. At first, I heard his dialogue as "religious stories" about Jesus coming to the earth so that he could die for my sins. But, the more he explained the more it became real to me. This story began to take on life and become personal to me. I thought to myself, *Really? Do you mean that God doesn't hate me? Is it true that God would help me?* When Zach asked me to pray with him, that one glimmer of hope was present in my heart. *If God would really help me, I need help.* I prayed his prayer, repeating after Zach the words of repentance. I didn't feel any different. I didn't have that silly smile on my face that Bo had come home from church with. I said goodbye to Zach in the hallway.

Next, I did what any junkie would do. I went to the bathroom downstairs in the emergency room waiting area. I locked the door. I mixed up the cocaine in the cap of my syringe. I searched in the dimness of the bathroom light for a vein and pushed in the plunger. I waited for the trains, the sound of the blood rushing past your eardrums as the cocaine accelerates your heart. There was nothing. I felt absolutely nothing. Maybe, God heard my prayer and was holding me to my words of commitment. I cleaned up and returned to the waiting room.

I was too high on these different drugs to show any authentic emotion. It is no wonder that Bo's family were distancing themselves from me. It is no surprise that Bo's mom started thinking that I had something to do with him dying. I can't remember if I cried. I don't know if I looked sad. I was numb. My memories of this time are sketchy and focused around drugs. It is as if I wasn't there for half of this nightmare.

When we turned off the machines, the family was gathered together in the room. I remember the moment but I can't remember showing any emotion. When the machine ceased breathing for Bo, it was the last breath he took. I'm not sure how long we sat in that room saying our goodbyes. I remember that I was the last to leave. I sat next to his body trying to grasp the fact that those eyes would never open again. I lifted the sheet that was draped over his body and tried to memorize every scar and every tattoo. I held his hand and wondered, *What do you want me to do now, Bo? Just tell me what to do.*

NINE

JESUS CAME WALKING IN MY GRAVEYARD

When he saw Jesus from afar....

Mark 5:6

Up until this point, I only thought that my life was out of control. After Bo's death, my life had no direction. Bo had been the voice that told me what to do and how to get it done. All of the animosity that I felt over the years was really masking the fact that I had no life outside of Bo. I didn't know how to think for myself or take care of myself. I was so lost.

Would you think I was crazy if I told you, I don't know what I did that night after Bo left this world. I don't know if I went home with his family or if I went to get high. I really don't remember. I don't remember telling my children that their father was gone. Jessica remembers that Pat, Melissa, and I sat all of the kids (Jessica, Hoss, and their two cousins) down in a circle and tried to explain that their daddy would never come back. I don't know how long my children cried or who wiped away their tears.

The next memory that I have was in the funeral home. I thought to myself, *I can't take this. I can't make it through this unless I get something to help me.* I placed a call from the funeral home to the doctor who prescribed the Adavans, and he called in a prescription for me. Dawn, the girl who had visited me in the hospital, showed up with a Dilaudid, and I shot up in the funeral home restroom.

Someone brought the children to the funeral home, and we took them in to see Bo's body. This is the first time I can remember seeing how my children were taking the loss of their father. I was so selfish and focused on how this was affecting my life that I wasn't thinking about helping my children or anyone else in the family through this moment. Jessica had always been a "daddy's girl." She was six- years -old and very grown-up. While her brother was too young to comprehend the brevity of the moment, Jessica was old enough to understand that daddy wasn't coming back. When Jessica was brought into the room and led up to the casket, she reached into the casket to touch Bo's face and began to scream in anger, "That is not my daddy! You're lying! That is not him!" The funeral director closed the sliding partition to stop anyone else from entering the viewing area as the whole family stood there in shock. I pulled Jessica's hand away as she was hitting Bo's face and smearing the makeup that had been applied by the people who had prepared his body. Gently, the funeral director suggested that everyone step out and they would fix the damage. We tried to explain the Jessica that this was her daddy's body but she loudly refused to accept. Someone took the kids back home, and I don't remember seeing them again for a few days.

I wish that someone would have shook me, screamed at me, and told me to get a grip on reality. Why didn't someone stop me? Instead, the family began to resent me. When I walked into the room where all of the family was gathered, I felt cold stares and heard faint whispers. I can't blame them. I was stoned and drugged out during my husband's wake and things got worse on the day of the funeral service.

The funeral home was packed. The word had spread far and wide about Bo's death and many people had come to pay their last respects. We were all dressed in our best black apparel. I had a black skirt and my high-heeled, black, leather boots.

Word was brought to me that Allen had shown up. Allen was the one who had been driving the car during the robberies and had turned states evidence against Bo. I became furious. I went marching through the funeral home to find him.

You could hear me screaming. "Where is he? How dare he show his face here?" When I found him, he very respectfully apologized and began to share his condolences. But, I was fit to be tied! I lit into him, scratching, clawing and kicking like a banshee! He calmly said, "I understand. I'll go. I'm sorry. I don't want to cause trouble." That didn't change anything. As he walked out of the building and to his car, I kicked him in the rear end every step of the way. I broke the heel off of my right boot. That poor guy!

When he drove off, the director of the funeral home approached me and said, "If you don't get control of yourself, you are going to have to leave. We need to get started." I squared my shoulders, looked him in the eyes, and said, "I'm ready to start." On the way back in the funeral home, I picked up the broken heel of my boot and found my seat.

After the funeral, I went with Dawn and got another Dilaudid. When I went back to Anne's house, all of the flowers from the funeral were on her front porch. I went inside, but everything felt different. I didn't feel like I belonged there anymore. I didn't want to sleep in the bed where Bo had died. I didn't know what to say to anybody. When they asked me, "What are you going to do?" I couldn't answer.

The only thing I had done for the past eight years on a consistent basis was to get high. I didn't know any other pattern of life. I had never made any plans for my life beyond tomorrow. I wasn't a good mother. I was a prostitute and a junkie. So, I did the only thing I knew how to do. I kept getting high.

My life was chaos. I didn't know where I was half of the time. I tried to go to the places that we used to go and realized that those were his friends. They weren't my friends. I didn't fit in there without him. I was so alone with nowhere to turn. I didn't talk to my mother. I hadn't spoken to my father since we left Florida with his money. I hadn't spoken to my brother since I ran away from home. I had no relationship with my children. The only family that I had known for the last eight years was Bo's family and I had ruined that as well.

Anne asked me to sign the life insurance policy that she was taking out on me. She had a small life insurance policy on Bo that had covered his funeral expenses. I didn't want to leave anyone with the burden of burying me if I died. She, also, convinced me to sign custody of the children over to her. I agreed with her, it would probably be best.

I went to the bar where my friend supplied me with coke. Eventually, I was staying there every night. He was supplying me with plenty of cocaine and letting me buy some Dilaudid, too. It was in the back of this bar that I died. I had been doing cocaine for three days and nights nonstop. I hadn't eaten or had anything to drink. It was midmorning on a Sunday, and the bar hardly had any customers. I begged for more cocaine and convinced him to make it a bigger piece because I wasn't "feeling" it. That should have been a signal. But, junkies don't think rationally. I mixed a shot, larger than usual and found a vein. I barely loosened the belt around my arm when the freight trains exploded in my head and I lost consciousness. As I died, it was different than the numbness I had felt in my first cocaine overdose. I was aware of my surroundings. I was very afraid. I stood in front of a skull, not a skeleton. It was a giant skull. Hands of darkness were reaching for me, pulling at me, trying to draw me into death. But, I turned and ran with all of my might. I ran back to my body. When I reached my body, I kept running. I ran out of the bar and down the street before I slowed down. With blood dripping from my arm, and a soft rain pelting my face, I realized that Hell was a real place and I didn't want to go there.

Before this moment in my life, I didn't care about dying. I felt as if I was living in hell on earth. I didn't think that heaven was a possibility for me. I didn't know that God would forgive me of my sins. When Zach explained salvation to me in the chapel of the hospital, it was the first time that I had heard the truth about God in a way that I could understand it. When I had attended church with my grandparents, I never grasped the concept that everyone has sinned and needs the forgiveness that Jesus' blood can provide. When I went to church with my friend, I didn't hear the plan of salvation. I had fun and sang songs but never grasped the truth about God.

I went back to Anne's house and told her what had happened. I don't think she took me serious. By now they were kind of put out with me. I went to the evening service at the church where Bo had gotten saved. I sat on the front row waiting for the sermon to be over. When he opened for prayer, I jumped up to talk to him. He asked me what I needed prayer for and I answered. "I died today and went to Hell. I need help." There was a prayer and as quick as it started it was over. I walked into the parking lot disappointed that I didn't have any direction.

I decided that I needed to get off of drugs and found out about a government program through my friends. This program supplied methadone to help you get off of heroin or Dilaudid. The only catch to this program was that I had to travel to Chattanooga every day for two or three weeks to pick up the methadone. My friends were carpooling down together. We had to meet early in the morning and drive to Chattanooga to be there when the clinic opened.

Methadone messed me up! I totaled three cars and don't remember where I left them. I passed out naked in someone's house and was draped across a chair when his parents and his three-year-old son came in. But, I was trying to clean myself up. I bought a Bible. It cost me a quarter at the thrift store. It was a worn Bible with a faded white cover. But, it reminded me of when I was little and still innocent. I tried to read it because I wanted God's help. Usually, I nodded off after just a few minutes. I would wake back up and try again. I sat there with that Bible, nodding for hours, and never successfully read the pages.

Zach's wife, Dara, had dropped by or called Anne's house and left a number if I ever wanted to call. I called them about three or four in the morning and talked for hours. They invited me to attend a revival with them. I didn't know what a "revival" was. I went to church with them and nodded through the first night. Although I don't remember much more about that night, I was told that I had a conversation with the preacher's wife. Evidently, I cussed her out when she was trying to pray for me and talk to me about how I was doing. I don't remember at all. I was loaded by the heavy doses of methadone and slept like a rock.

Zach and Dara offered to let me stay with them for a while under certain conditions. I couldn't tell anyone where I was. I couldn't bring anyone over to the house. I agreed to their conditions and slept on their couch. I discovered later that they stayed up throughout the night praying over me to be free from the addiction. I went back to the revival with them the next night. I fell asleep again during the sermon. This time the preacher came over, shook me, and woke me up. He said, "Do you really want help, girl?" For that one moment it seemed as if I was in my right mind. I stood to my feet and answered him. "Yes sir, I do." He reached out to pray for me and I went down. I'm not sure how long I was on the floor. When I got to my feet, I whispered to Dara. "I think that man knocked me down. Did you see him knock me down?"

Then, I realized that I felt more sober than I had in eight years. My mind was clear and I could actually think. I felt free! Jesus came walking in my graveyard. He set me free from the inner destruction that had caused me separation from my family and destruction of my life. I gave my life to God that night, August 10th, 1992. When I went home to Zach and Daira's house, I flushed my pot and my pills down the drain.

TEN

CLOTHED AND IN MY RIGHT MIND

Then they came to Jesus, and saw the one who had been demon-possessed and had the legion, sitting and clothed and in his right mind. Mark 5:15

I am not sure that I had ever been in "my right mind" before this point in my life. Before the addiction, the prostitution, the abuse, the shame and the failures, I wasn't in a "right mind." I could face my life with the ability to make right choices.

My perception was free of the gloom and the despair that I had been enslaved with. I saw hope for my future. I began to slowly rebuild my life. The revival at the church was going on every night. I took my Bible and followed along with the preachers, soaking up God's Word like a sponge. Buddy and Jeanne Steele were the preachers holding the meetings, and they were both animated and exciting to listen to. Buddy Steele was funny one minute and strong the next. Jeanne would start preaching and it seemed like the momentum built like a freight train. I learned so much and I had so much that I needed to learn.

Zach and Daira were so patient with me. I knew absolutely nothing about God or the Bible. I didn't know how to shop or keep house. I didn't know how to pay bills or get up before noon. I had to learn everything about being responsible. My lessons started right away as Daira took me to put in applications for a job. I had not worked a regular job since I was a waitress at sixteen-years-old. So, I went to the restaurants. I was hired at the O'Charley's Restaurant near Rivergate Mall. Since I didn't have any money, they helped me buy the necessary clothes for my uniform and gave me a ride everyday.

My next lesson in responsibility was my car. The car I had been driving was not legal. I had bought the car on payments from an individual who I had met under illegal circumstances. He disappeared and I had no title. Zach tried to help me search for the title so I could locate the owner. The vehicle registration number came back as stolen. I had been driving a stolen car! Needless to say, I couldn't drive it anymore.

I set up a meeting with Bo's family and invited my mom and Jim to attend. Zach and Daira went with me to share the great news of my freedom. The enthusiasm for my great transformation was not reciprocated from any of the family. I told them that I was clean, had a job, and wanted to raise my kids. I thought that they would be pleased. I thought that they would want my kids to have a regular home with their mother. They had no intention of returning the custody of my children to me. They said that they didn't expect my transformation to last. After that meeting, I became the enemy to Bo's family for quite some time.

My previous method of response when things got tough was quit or run. But I wasn't who I used to be. I wasn't the messed up failure anymore. I found out that I was a new creation. I found myself in Second Corinthians 5:17, "Therefore, if anyone *is* in Christ, *he is* a new creation; old things have passed away; behold, all things have become new." My mind was changed by the truths I was learning from God's instruction manual. I faced this mess I had made with hope and a lot of encouragement and prayer from the people in the church.

I went to the courts to find out what it would take to get custody of my children returned to me. Bo's family pointed out to the judge my long history of addiction, my arrest record, my lack of a legal driver's license, and my lack of a home. They even brought an entourage of people to testify against me. The judge shocked us all by her stern response, "I'm not interested in what Michelle did in the past. I want to know what Michelle is doing right now." Right then, I knew that God was on my side. I walked into that courtroom hoping for God's mercy, and I knew I had just witnessed the favor of God.

The judge granted me an attorney/mediator who reviewed my case and set up supervised visitation at Anne's house. The mediator explained what the judge would want me to accomplish to show that I was ready and able to take care of my children. This included having a home suitable for the children and me, having a legal driver's license, passing required drug screenings, and having a consistent work record. This long list of requirements seemed like a lot for a person as irresponsible as I had been. I am sure that Bo's family didn't think I could pull it off. I was willing to do my part. I also believed that God wanted me to have my children and would help me by doing the things that I was incapable of doing.

I began researching what it would take to get my driver's license back. I discovered that I had nearly two thousand dollars in fines and tickets. There was a judgment against me from a car wreck for nearly three thousand dollars. I needed a SR-22 insurance. In addition, the fee to reinstate my license was almost one thousand dollars. This looked impossible. I hung up the phone after gathering all of the information, and my heart began to sink. I didn't make enough money as a waitress to pay for all of these fines and fees and still get an apartment before the required deadline. I put a coin in the payphone and called Pastor Jeanne from the church. I didn't want to open my mouth and ruin everything I had prayed by telling how I felt and what my circumstance looked like. I simply said, "Please speak some faith to me." She began declaring God's report. "My God shall supply all your need according to his riches in glory. God owns the cattle on a thousand hills. You are the head and not the tail." She spoke to me for five minutes about God's faithfulness. I was in a faith fight. I was fighting for my children for the first time in life.

To my surprise, the attorney who was my mediator was able to get the judgment reduced and had the majority of the fines and tickets erased. I rejoiced and shouted all over the place.

God's favor was working on my behalf! I experienced unnatural favor even more as people from the church and at my job began giving me money to help. I waited on a table of five businessmen who left me an hundred dollar bill as my tip. It took a few months, but I was able to obtain my driver's license before the next court appearance.

During this time, I had scheduled supervised visits with my children. The first visit didn't happen because I was five minutes late. Zach and Daira were responsible to drive me everywhere. They picked me up from work in Goodlettsville and we rushed to East Nashville in the midst of afternoon traffic. We arrived at Anne's house five minutes past the time that the court ordered visit was supposed to begin. When I went to the door Anne barely opened the door. She informed me that since I was late she wasn't going to let me have the visit. My little boy saw me through the crack in the door and came running to hug me. Anne pushed him behind her and told him, "No, you can't see her." She shut the door in my face and left me with tears running down my face.

I have to admit that I was confused by her behavior. When Bo was alive, we took the kids whenever we wanted and kept them as long as we wanted. During that time, everybody knew we were either drinking or getting high. Here I was living clean and sober, actually working a job, and trying to live a normal life. But, she wouldn't even let me in the house. I didn't argue. The next day I called my mediator who contacted Anne's lawyer. I made sure that I was early for the next visit.

Anne never made the visits comfortable. She didn't speak to me. Her house was always full of other hostile family who glared at me as I walked in and as I walked out. I was escorted back to a small room that doubled as the laundry room and the toy room. I was there for four hours a week. I learned how to play with them and keep their attention. I probably spent more quality time with them each week during those visits than I ever had given them on a regular basis.

Years later, Anne told me that she was testing me. She wanted to see how bad I really wanted my kids. She surely put me to the test. She made me walk the line. I'm glad for it today. I discovered how valuable my relationship with my children really was. I found out that being a good mother required that I become unselfish. I had to put their stability and security above my needs or feelings.

By the time I returned for the custody hearing, I had passed every random drug test, obtained my legal driver's license, received a reference from my employer for steady work, and moved in to a two bedroom apartment. None of these things happened in the blink of an eye. Each thing seemed to drag out and run up to the last minute. The apartment was rented the day before I was scheduled for the social worker's inspection. The people from my church brought furniture and dishes, towels and toys. Within twenty-four hours I went from sleeping on Daira's couch with minimal belongings to having my own fully furnished apartment. This was the nicest, cleanest place that I had ever lived. I had beds, a couch, and even pictures on my wall! Serving Jesus Christ was causing my life to be stable in a way that it had never been before!

I was granted custody of my children with no hesitation. In the courtroom, Anne told the judge that she would gladly watch the children while I worked. I agreed, and we worked a price that I could afford. My kids were happy to be with me. They still visited Anne and the rest of their family every week. My mom and Jim came to church with us and we went out as a family every week to dinner.

We settled in to our busy life with church, work, and the kids. Jessica was involved in a dance and twirling group. We dressed her in the sequins and lace, and she twirled her baton. She was precious. At the suggestion of my mom and Jim, I started calling my son Gene instead of Hoss. They argued that having a nickname like "Hoss" might cause some fights or harassment in school. I could see their point. He wasn't big enough to be a "Hoss." His real name was Earl Eugene Cosby III. When he tried to tell someone his real name "the third" came out as "the turd." He was only five. My dad's name is Gene and my middle name is Jean. So, Hoss became Gene.

ELEVEN

LEAVING THE GRAVEYARD

"Do not fear, for you will not be ashamed;
neither be disgraced, for you will not be put to
shame; For you will forget the shame of your
youth, and will not remember the reproach of
your widowhood anymore." Isaiah 54:4

This verse became such an inspiration to me.
As I would read this verse, I could see that God
wanted me to have a life that was complete. God
wanted to move me from the place of desolation to
a life that had stability and fullness. The first step
to this new future was to deal with fear. Fear had

been a part of my life ever since I could remember. I began to target the areas of fear and resist them.

Thoughts of fear are so real that even your physical body responds to them. Even if the thoughts have no basis in reality, your body can act as if they are true facts. The most vivid memory I have that I could use to describe this to you is driving. For eight years, I had been terrified every time that a police car got in the lane behind me. Either my tags belonged to another car, my insurance was expired, my license was revoked, or I had drugs in the car. So, now that I was drug free and legal, I had nothing to worry about. Still, whenever a police car would pull in behind me, my hands began to sweat, my stomach got butterflies and I glanced nervously to the rearview mirror. I caught myself one day and said out loud, "I am legal to drive. I have insurance. There are no drugs in my car. Why am I feeling this way?" I realized that fear had become a habit in my life.

I became conscious of the battle that was taking place in my mind. I recognized that when I drove by certain intersections or saw certain objects that reminded me of my drug activity, my mind would be bombarded with suggestions and bad ideas. God's Word was showing me that I didn't have to take every thought that came my way. As a matter of fact, I was responsible to "cast down imaginations" and "take thoughts captive." I began quoting something that I had studied from the Bible when those thoughts attacked my mind. I discovered that I had to use the weapon of the Word in the same manner that Jesus had used this weapon. When the devil attacked Jesus, he opened his mouth and quoted what God had said.

In learning how to pray, I found out that I needed to use the Word of God as my basis. If I could find it in the Word, then it was the will of God for my life. I began to pray about the man I wanted to marry. I went to the Word to make my list of characteristics that I wanted in a man. Some of the things that I was asking God for were: a man stronger in his walk with God than I was; a man who praised God louder than me, a man who would love my children as his own; etc.

There were a couple of guys in the church who were interested in me. But, they didn't qualify according to my prayer list. I wanted God's will for my life, and I wasn't interested in wasting time on any one who wasn't what I was praying for. The pastors had a son who was moving from Kansas City following a failed marriage. I wasn't considering him as even being a possibility because of the turmoil of his situation. But, God had other plans. I remember the first week that he was in Nashville. I heard God speak to my heart that if I was willing to believe, I could have Philip as my husband. I shook my head and thought, *Is that just me or was that really you, God?* I felt that reassurance again in my heart. If I would believe, I could marry Philip Steele.

I hid this in my heart for a few weeks. I prayed about it and searched my heart. I wanted God's perfect will for my life. I began to get bold in my prayer. One day, I became so bold that as I was shaking hands with Philip on the front stairs of the church I asked him, "Did you know that you are my miracle?" Each time that we met, our handshakes were long and our eye contact spoke words that we couldn't say.

My faith and patience was rewarded when I became Mrs. Philip Steele almost a year later. We never dated before our wedding. I wanted this marriage to be built on integrity and God's righteousness. Other than phone conversations and long handshakes in the church, we stayed apart.

Philip truly is the man of my dreams. His walk with God is an ongoing inspiration to me. When we first married, we both had many areas of our lives that needed to mature and grow. My husband has proven his integrity and gained my respect as I have watched him grow and become a man of strength in God's Word. He taught me how to say, "I'm sorry." He has helped me learn to walk by faith. He is the most honorable man I know.

My children were thrilled to have Philip as their new father and began calling him "Daddy" right away. My prayer has been answered, as over the years Philip has loved my children as his own. He has never called them "stepchildren." He has provided for them in every way-spiritually, physically and emotionally.

TWELVE

THE SERMON FROM THE GRAVEYARD

*And he departed, and began to publish in
Decapolis how great*
*things Jesus had done for him; and all men did
marvel.* MARK 5:20

*Yea, I will rejoice over them to do them good,
and I will plant them*
*in this land assuredly with my whole heart
and with my whole soul.*
JEREMIAH 32:41

If you had asked me during my B.C. days -my days before Christ-if I could imagine myself as a person who taught the Bible, I would have laughed out loud. About three weeks after I was saved, as the preacher was praying for me, he said that my testimony would go around the world. That was the first indication that I would be used to do something great for God.

What an honor and a privilege to give something back to the One who saved my life from destruction! I started by sharing my testimony and singing in church. Over the years, God has equipped me to teach, preach and write for his kingdom. As I proved myself faithful over one area of responsibility, God would trust me with something else.

My husband and I moved to the Kansas City area for the purpose of being closer to his son. Philip landed a job in a billing division of a large insurance company and moved up the ladder. I became pregnant with my daughter, Angela who was born on June 26, 1995. Philip and I attended church regularly and volunteered in many capacities. My husband served as an assistant pastor for some time and saw God move greatly through his ministry. We became the senior pastors of Faith Builders International around 1998. Since that time we have seen God expand our ministry in awesome ways.

We developed relationships through which God has poured into our lives. Pastors E.C. and Inez Morton have been a source of stability and encouragement in our lives that is priceless. Pastor Happy Caldwell and his wife, Jeanne, are a constant source of strength and faith as I watch their resolve to remain steadfast to God's purpose despite the adversities. I want that same longevity in my ministry.

Through these great men and women, I have discovered that God wants to do me good! At the onset of this chapter, I shared my favorite scripture with you. In this verse, it is God speaking. He says that he wants to do us good! I found out how to be in a position to receive this "good." I have to be in a position of obedience. When I obey God, He can do "good" in my life. I had to cut up my "American Excuse" card and obey what God wanted for my life. I couldn't use the excuse of my past, my failures, or my shame. I had to step up and preach God's Word.

God has honored me with great opportunities. My books and CDs have touched lives around the world. I have ministered on television, in prisons, in great churches and conferences. I teach in our Bible College and pastor the greatest church in the world. I love to go walking in the graveyard and free people from addiction, depression, and any bondage that keeps them from experiencing God's best.

I have experienced one vision thus far in my life. In this vision, I stood on a small pedestal dressed in my filthy rags. As I spoke to people and showed these rags, I was capturing their attention. The instant that I had their attention, I would point them to Jesus Christ who stood on a pedestal much higher than mine. I knew that the dirty rags represented the experiences of my past. I have attempted to be as transparent as I possibly could. At the same time, I have tried not to sound "churchy." I want to point you to Jesus Christ.

If you don't know the freedom that I have described, you can know this freedom by making Jesus the Lord of your life. His presence in your life will bring the stability and strength to your life that ensures a life that is worth living.

You can pray this prayer for salvation. Don't just read it. Open your heart and speak this forth from your mouth. When you pray this prayer from a sincere heart, you will be born again:

Heavenly Father, in the Name of Jesus, I present myself to you. I pray and ask Jesus to be Lord over my life. I believe it in my heart, so I say it with my mouth: "Jesus has been raised from the dead." This moment, I make Him the Lord over my life. Jesus, come into my heart. I believe this moment that I am saved, I say it now: "I am reborn. I am a Christian. I am a child of Almighty God."

This is the beginning. You need to grow. That means you will need a church where you can learn how to walk with God. God's Word will be your strength and your weapon. So, get a Bible and read it.

If you need prayer or you want to share your testimony with me, you can contact me through my church or the website. I'd love to hear from you.

For more information or for prayer:

Michelle Steele Ministries
Faith Builders International
PO Box 452
De Soto, KS 66018

Office -913-583-1670
Toll-free- 1-888-901-8242

www.michellesteeleministries.com

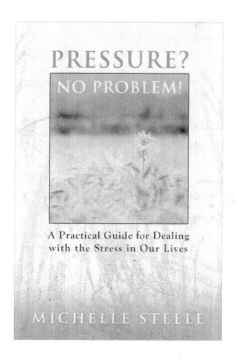

Pressure? No Problem!
The pressure you are facing today has a purpose. It has come to steal your peace, paralyze your faith and hinder your progress. It is designed by your adversary to wear you down, make you weary, and cause you to quit. The enemy wants to make you change your mind. But God is on your side! He has equipped you to rise above the resistance and defeat the pressure.
Soft-cover book $12

Now You See Me Now You Don't
Life may have positioned you in a pit. The situation may
have you in a stranglehold. Your past may be holding you
hostage. Your present circumstance may be threatening to
break you. Find out how you can soar above the storm and
break free from the barriers in your life. It isn't a magic
trick. It is not an illusion. It is a transformation. In her book
"Now You See Me, Now You Don't!" Michelle Steele will
equip you to leave the situation and enter the revelation!
Soft-cover book $12

The Guilt, The Shame and The Blood
The Guilt: I wasn't trying to hide the fact I was guilty. I
was trying to forget about it. But, every time the drugs
wore off, there was more shame to remind me.
The Shame: No one else could see the shame that haunted
me. Everyone could see the results of the self-destruction
that shame was producing in my life. Someone else was
raising my children. My body was for sale every night.
Addiction was my prison and my escape.
The Blood: Then, I found the blood that removed my guilt .
. .
Soft-cover book $12

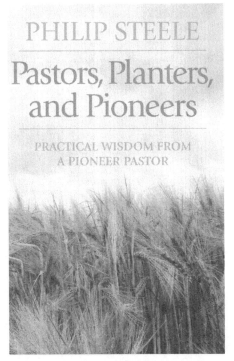

Pastors, Planters and Pioneers
Pastor Philip Steele

Planting churches is a biblical mandate and will result in people's lives being changed and them ultimately making a difference in the world. John 20:21 "Then said Jesus to them again, Peace be unto you: as my Father hath sent me, even so send I you. Go into every man's world and make disciples, baptize and teach." Learn to release the destiny within through Pastors, Planters and Pioneers!
Soft-cover book $12